LIGHTNING
BOLT
BOOKS™

Can You Tell a Dolphin from a Porpoise?

Buffy Silverman

Lerner Publications Company
Minneapolis

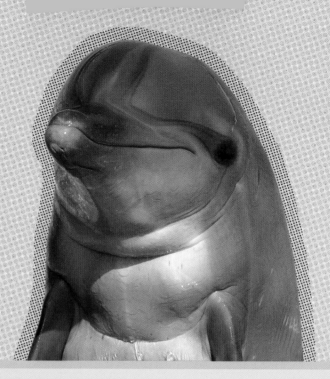

Lerner Publications Company
A division of Lerner Publishing Group, Inc.
241 First Avenue North
Minneapolis, MN 55401 U.S.A.

Website address: www.lernerbooks.com

Library of Congress Cataloging-in-Publication Data

Silverman, Buffy.
    Can you tell a dolphin from a porpoise? / by Buffy Silverman.
        p.   cm. — (Lightning bolt books™—Animal look-alikes)
    Includes index.
    ISBN 978-0-7613-6734-5 (lib. bdg. : alk. paper)
    1. Dolphins—Juvenile literature. 2. Porpoises—Juvenile literature. I. Title.
    QL737.C432S5386 2012
    599.53—dc22   2010052814

Manufactured in the United States of America
1 — CG — 7/15/11

Contents

Pointed or Round

Dolphins and porpoises look a lot alike. Their smooth shape lets them glide through ocean water. A few swim in rivers.

This porpoise's smooth body helps it move through the water.

This bottlenose dolphin is a mammal. People are mammals too.

These animals are not fish. They are mammals. Like all mammals, dolphins and porpoises feed their babies milk. They breathe air.

But you can tell these animals apart. Look at this dolphin's head. Its snout has a pointed beak. The beak sticks out in front.

A porpoise does not have a pointed beak. Its snout is smaller and curved.

This harbor porpoise shows off its curved snout.

When a dolphin opens its beak, you see its many sharp teeth. The teeth are shaped like cones.

A porpoise has fewer teeth inside its mouth. Its teeth are shaped like pointed shovels. They are flatter than a dolphin's teeth. But they are still sharp.

Built to Swim

Dolphins and porpoises are built for swimming. They move their tails up and down. Their powerful tails push them through water. Strong tails also launch them into the air.

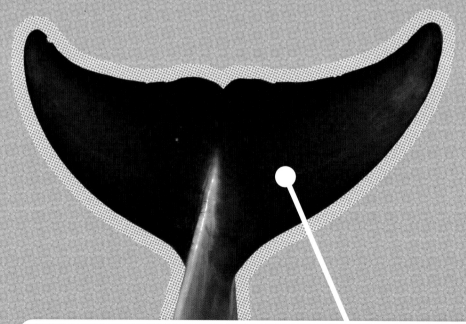

A dolphin's tail sticks up as the animal dives back down into the water.

A dolphin's body is long and sleek. Imagine a tall person lying down. A small dolphin is about that long. Some dolphins grow much bigger.

An orca is the largest kind of dolphin. It is as long as a small fishing boat.

Porpoises have shorter, fatter bodies.

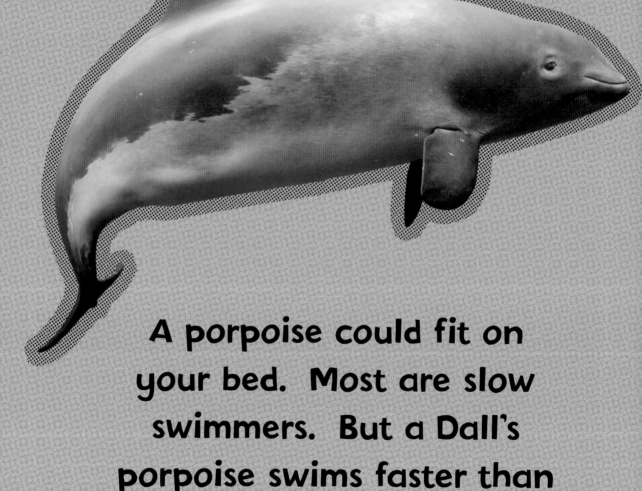

A porpoise could fit on your bed. Most are slow swimmers. But a Dall's porpoise swims faster than the speediest dolphin!

Two flippers help dolphins and porpoises steer. They move their flippers to twist and turn. Quick turns keep them from crashing when they swim in a crowd.

This dolphin uses its flippers and tail to twist out of the water.

A back fin helps dolphins and porpoises balance.
A porpoise's back fin is shaped like a triangle.

A dolphin's fin curves
backward. It is taller than
a porpoise's fin.

These taller, curved
fins belong to dolphins.

Both animals have an opening called a blowhole on top of their heads. This lets them breathe air. They open the blowhole at the water's surface, and air flows in. The blowhole closes when they dive down. Then they don't breathe in water.

This hole allows a porpoise to breathe.

Living in Groups

Dolphins and porpoises swim in groups. The group is called a pod. Adults in a pod keep the young safe. They watch out for animals that may eat the young or other group members.

Porpoise pods are usually small.

Ten or fewer porpoises form a pod.

Some dolphin pods are huge.
Thousands of dolphins may
live together in one pod.

Dolphins like to
be around lots of
other dolphins.

19

Pod members work together to find food. Dolphins often follow fishing boats. They snatch fish from the boats' nets.

These dolphins are not afraid to swim close to boats.

Porpoises don't usually follow boats. **They are shy.** They stay away from people.

People see porpoises less often than dolphins. Porpoises usually swim far from boats and people.

Finding Food

Dolphins and porpoises are predators. They hunt other animals for food. They eat fish, shrimp, squid, and crayfish. Their teeth grip their catch. But they do not chew their food. They swallow it whole.

Porpoises usually hunt in shallow water. A porpoise pod swims around a group of fish, called a school. They surround the school and trap it. Each porpoise takes a turn swimming through the school and eating.

Porpoises swim in shallow water to hunt fish.

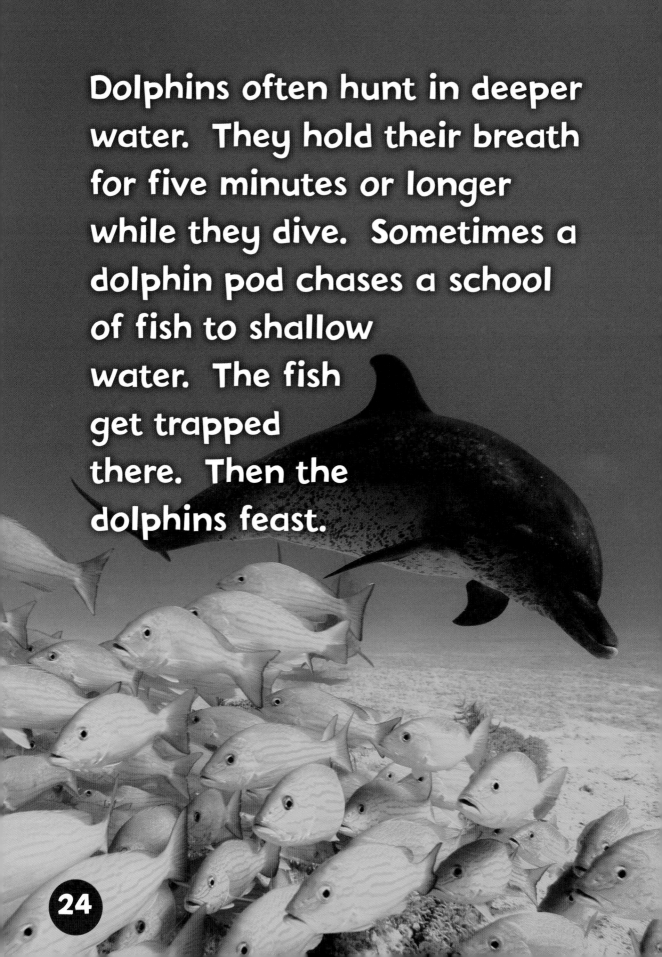

Dolphins often hunt in deeper water. They hold their breath for five minutes or longer while they dive. Sometimes a dolphin pod chases a school of fish to shallow water. The fish get trapped there. Then the dolphins feast.

How do dolphins and porpoises find food in dark waters? They have a special sense called echolocation. They click and whistle. Their sounds bounce off other swimming animals.

This porpoise uses echolocation to find fish in the dark.

This dolphin found a good meal!

Then the dolphins and porpoises listen to the echoes. The echoes tell them where something is. They tell them if a school of fish is large or small.

Dolphins and porpoises leap
and dive in oceans.

Can you tell these
look-alikes apart?

Who Am I?

Look at the pictures below. Which ones are dolphins? Which ones are porpoises?

 My tall fin curves backward.

My back fin looks like a triangle.

 I am shy. I swim in a small group.

I leap and dive near boats and people.

 I have no beak. My head is rounded.

My pointed beak sticks out in front.

Fun Facts

- Dolphins and porpoises don't curl up in bed at night as you do. They rest while they swim. Part of their brain stays alert. Their brain tells them when it is time to surface and breathe.

- Dall's porpoises are one of the fastest mammals in water. They can swim 35 miles (56 kilometers) per hour.

- Many porpoises and dolphins can hold their breath for 7 to 10 minutes. A pilot whale is a kind of dolphin. It can hold its breath for 20 minutes.

- Some dolphins slap the water around fish to make bubbles. The fish are afraid of the bubbles and won't swim through them, so they get trapped. Then the dolphins eat them.

Glossary

beak: the pointy front part of a dolphin's head

blowhole: the opening on the back of a porpoise, dolphin, or whale. The animal breathes through this hole.

echolocation: a sense that dolphins and porpoises use to find food and other things. Dolphins and porpoises make sounds and listen to their echoes to tell the location of something.

fin: a thin structure on a dolphin's or porpoise's back that sticks up and helps the animal balance

flippers: a pair of limbs on a dolphin's or porpoise's sides that it uses to steer

mammal: an animal that makes milk to feed to its baby

predator: an animal that hunts and eats other animals

snout: the long front part of an animal's head, including its nose, mouth, and jaws

Further Reading

Harbor Porpoises—National Wildlife Federation http://www.nwf.org/Kids/Ranger-Rick/Animals/Mammals/Harbor-Porpoises.aspx

Hatkoff, Juliana, Isabella Hatkoff, and Craig Hatkoff. *Winter's Tail: How One Little Dolphin Learned to Swim Again.* New York: Scholastic Press, 2009.

Marine Mammals—Dall's Porpoise http://kids.nceas.ucsb.edu/mmp/Dall.html

National Geographic Animal Video: Dolphin Parenting http://video.nationalgeographic.com/video/player/animals/mammals-animals/dolphins-and-porpoises/dolphin_parenting.html

National Geographic Kids: The Secret Language of Dolphins http://kids.nationalgeographic.com/kids/stories/animalsnature/dolphin-language

Waxman, Laura Hamilton. *Diving Dolphins.* Minneapolis: Lerner Publications Company, 2003.

Index

Photo Acknowledgments

The images in this book are used with the permission of: © Tier und Naturfotografie/SuperStock, p. 1 (top); © Minden Pictures/SuperStock, pp. 1 (bottom), 23; © Brian J. Abela/Shutterstock Images, p. 2; © Florian Graner/SeaPics.com, p. 4; © Brandon Cole, pp. 5, 17; © Barry Brown/Visuals Unlimited, Inc., pp. 6, 28 (bottom/right); © Andrea Innocenti/CuboImages srl/Alamy, pp. 7, 28 (bottom/left); © Stephen Frink/CORBIS, p. 8; © Masa Ushioda/CoolWaterPhoto.com, p. 9; © Mauro Rodrigues/Shutterstock Images, p. 10; © George McCallum/SeaPics.com, p. 11; © Solvin Zankl/Visuals Unlimited, Inc., pp. 12, 27 (top); © Linda Thompson/Flickr/Getty Images, p. 13; © Fotosearch/SuperStock, pp. 14, 28 (top/right); © blickwinkel/NaturimBild/Alamy, pp. 15, 28 (top/left); © Erik Christensen/Wikimedia Foundation , Inc., p. 16; © Florian Graner/naturepl.com, pp. 18, 21, 25, 28 (middle/left); © DAJ/Getty Images, p. 19; © Megan Whittaker/Alamy, pp. 20, 28 (middle/right); © Juniors Bildarchiv/F282/Alamy, p. 22; © Hiroya Minakuchi/Minden Pictures, p. 24; © Norbert Wu/Minden Pictures, p. 26; © David Fleetham/Tom Stack & Associates, Inc., p. 27 (bottom); © Photo by China Photos/Getty Images, p. 30; © Hiroya Minakuchi/Minden Pictures/Getty Images, p. 31.

Front cover: © FGraner FGraner/Wildlife/Photolibrary (Harbor Porpoise); © Mike Hill/Photographer's Choice/Getty Images (Bottle-Nosed Dolphin).

Main body text set in Johann Light 30/36.